海达斯

原版英文手写笔记本

作者：

乔治·默瑟·道森

1878 年

封面和第 1-13 页以及第 68 页使用谷歌翻译从英文翻译而来。

原始笔记本是手写的英文。

资料来源：麦吉尔大学档案馆，魁北克省蒙特利尔，道森-**哈灵**顿档案 MG 1022。
https://digitalarchives.library.mcgill.ca/MUA/MG1022/series6/ mua_dawson_fonds_MUAMG1022-6-104.pdf **由加拿大渥太**华的

Peter D. Geldart **准**备， geldartp@gmail.com Petra Books MBO Coworking 78 George Street, Suite 204 Ottawa ON K1N 5W1

加拿大 封面：George Mercer Dawson **的地**图基于他 1878 **年**对夏洛特皇后群岛的调查。加拿大地质调查局，彩色地质图 139，1878 **年**。 **封面**图例： **深**绿色：中新世 **浅**绿色：白垩纪 **浅米色**：**集**块岩、灰岩，可能是三叠纪 **深米色**：**三叠**纪 红色：侵入花岗岩、闪长岩等。
https://open.library.ubc.ca/viewer/bcbooks/1.0222501#p288z-7r0f:map%20139

"**海达人的**习俗中，最令人称奇的，可能还带有某种宗教意义的是与舞蹈仪式有关的习俗。同样引人注目的是，据说这些习俗大多来自邻近大陆的齐姆西亚人，这群人说着一种截然不同的语言，并且曾与海达人发生过激烈的战争。" – 乔治·M·**道森 手稿第** 15 页

简介

“我介绍了一些有关岛上居民的非凡种族的细节，尽管他们可能是美国最有趣的原住民之一，但关于他们的准确信息却很少。”

– 乔治·M·道森

手稿第 2 页

这本由乔治·默瑟·道森 (GMD) 于 1849-1901 年撰写的笔记本最初由麦吉尔大学档案馆为道森-哈灵顿档案馆拍摄。在这本小册子中，为了确保最佳可读性，笔记本的每一页都分布在两页上。

“海达人”是一篇 1878 年的文章，包括他自己用铅笔编辑和评论。其中大部分内容由哈珀新月刊准备，并于 1880 年出版 - 但这份手写手稿中有 30% 是独一无二的，从未出版过。这也是他在编写加拿大地质调查局 (GSC) 出版的 1880 年皇后夏洛特群岛报告附录 A 和 B 时思考的一部分。请参阅参考资料。

1878 年至 1898 年，他探索了不列颠哥伦比亚省西北海岸，包括夏洛特皇后群岛 (Haida Gwaii)。“我们 [1878] 探险的目的是与加拿大地质调查局合作，对这些岛屿进行初步的地质、地理和总体勘探。”（手稿第 2 页）他曾担任该局的助理局长（1877-1895 年）和局长（1895-1901 年）。

他个人对“消失的印第安人”社区及其文化和语言的民族志研究很感兴趣。他经常会就这个主题写到深夜（他有点书呆子气）。他在维多利亚时代的蒙特利尔上流社会长大（他的父亲威廉爵士是麦吉尔大学的校长），受过良好的教育，英语很好，擅长素描和水彩画。我附上了他 1878 年笔记本中的素描，那一年他正在勘测夏洛特皇后群岛，尽管这些素描不是“海达人”笔记本的一部分。

因为他有驼背，土著人可能认为他“精神上”，许多人可能尊重他并让他加入他们中间。

“许多人都亲切地称他为‘小巨人’，而加拿大原住民则称他为‘Skookum Tumtum’，意为‘勇敢、快乐的人’……他的报告《加拿大印第安人过去和现在状况概述》在早期发展理解和尊重加拿大原住民方面具有特别重要的历史和文化意义。”参见 [https://archive.org/details/cihm_02365/page/n5/mode/2up]

– John Ashton, Saltwire，新格拉斯哥新闻，

新斯科舍省，2017 年 9 月 25 日。

“正是在不列颠哥伦比亚省，道森赢得了‘加拿大民族学最重要的贡献者之一’和‘加拿大人类学之父’的声誉……作为一名艺术家和诗人，他被海达图腾柱的美丽以及他们村庄建设所体现的智慧和技能所吸引。作为一名达尔文主义科学家，他察觉到了一种高度进化的文化……道森的开创性研究和奉献精神使国际社会关注到加拿大丰富的民族学遗产……并深深影响了这个国家人类学的理论和制度发展。”

– 苏珊娜· 泽勒和盖尔· 阿夫里斯–韦克姆

《加拿大传记词典》第十三卷。

GMD 于 1878

年绘制的素描未收录在《海达人》论文中，这本完整的笔记本是在他 1878 年调查夏洛特皇后群岛时写的，可在以下网址查看：
https://digitalarchives.library.mcgill.ca/MUA/MG1022/mua_george-mercer-dawson-diary_1878_envelope-49_MG1022.pdf

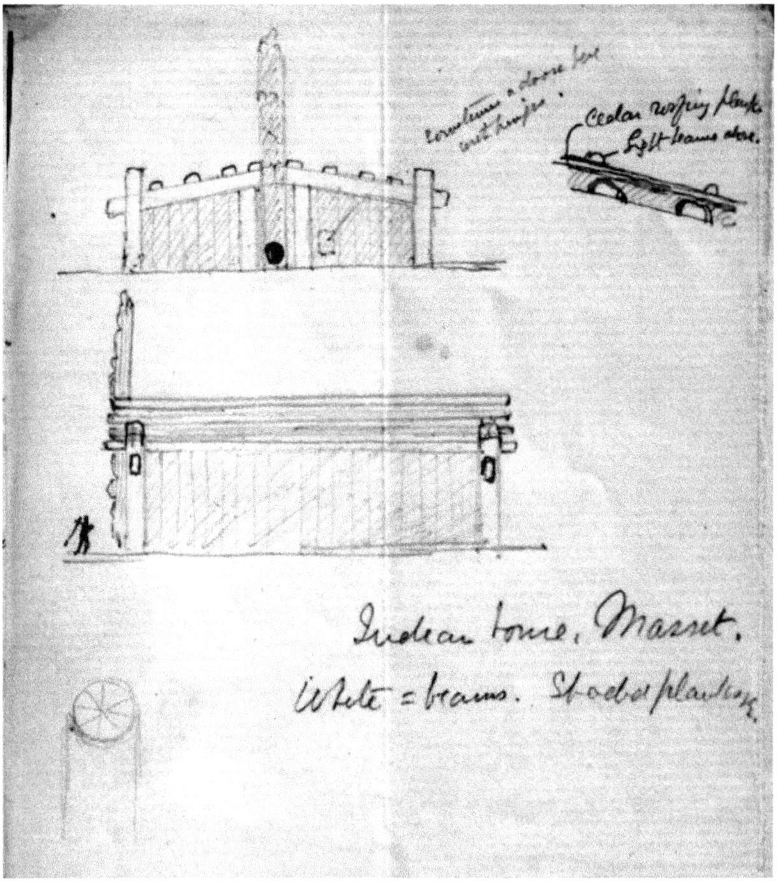

乔治·默瑟·道森 (George Mercer Dawson) 绘制的草图，夏洛特皇后群岛调查，1878 年。麦吉尔大学 mg1022 文件 134 第 5 页。

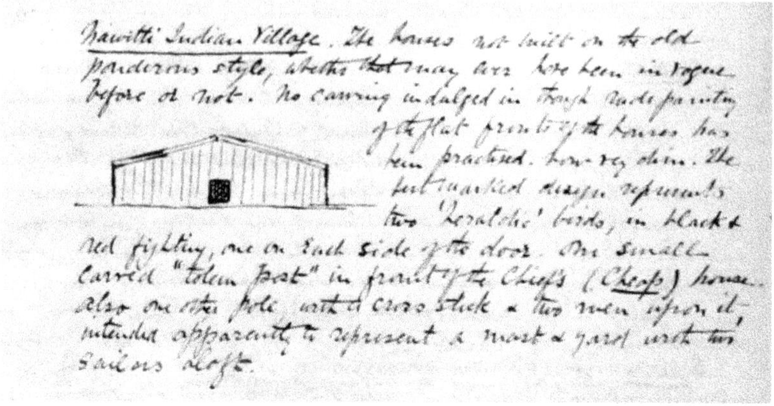
Nawitti Indian Village. The houses not built on the old ponderous style, whether that may are have been in vogue before or not. No carving indulged in though rude painting of the flat fronts of the houses has been practised. The first marked design represents two 'Xeralthie' birds, in black & red fighting, one on each side of the door. One small carved "totem post" in front of the Chief's (Cheap) house. also one other pole with a cross stick & two men upon it, intended apparently to represent a mast & yard with two sailors aloft.

乔治·**默瑟·道森**绘制的草图，夏洛特皇后群岛调查，1878 **年。麦吉**尔大学 mg1022 **文件** 134 **第** 192 页

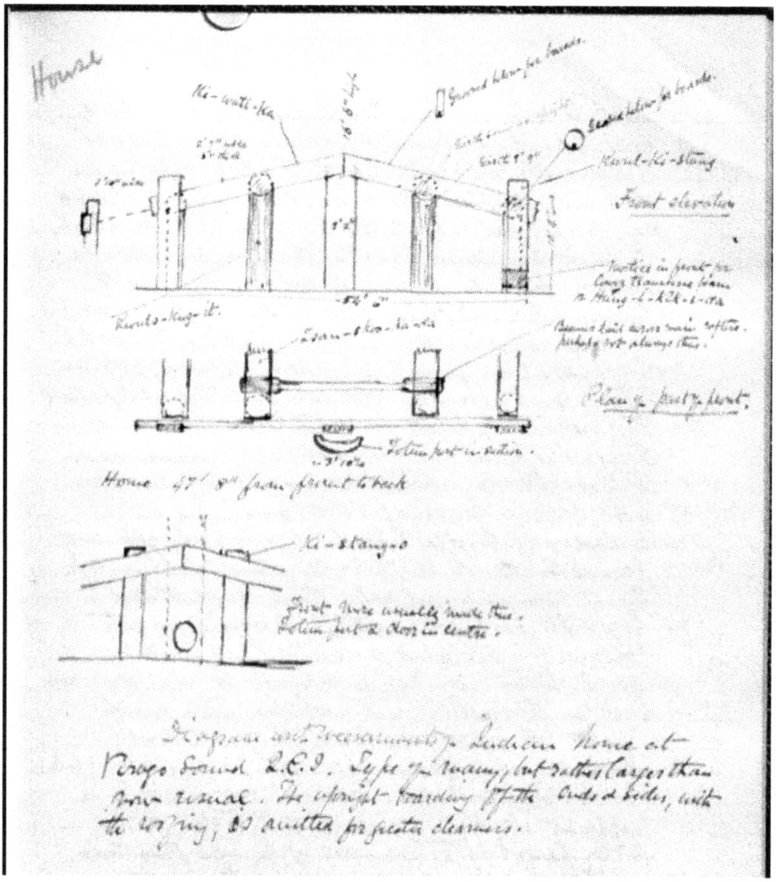

Diagram and measurements of Indian house at Virago Sound Q.C.I. Type of many but rather larger than usual. The upright boarding of the ends & sides, with the roofing, is omitted for greater clearness.

乔治·**默瑟·道森** (George Mercer Dawson) 绘制的草图，夏洛特皇后群岛调查，1878 **年。麦吉**尔大学 mg1022 **文件** 134 **第** 157 页。

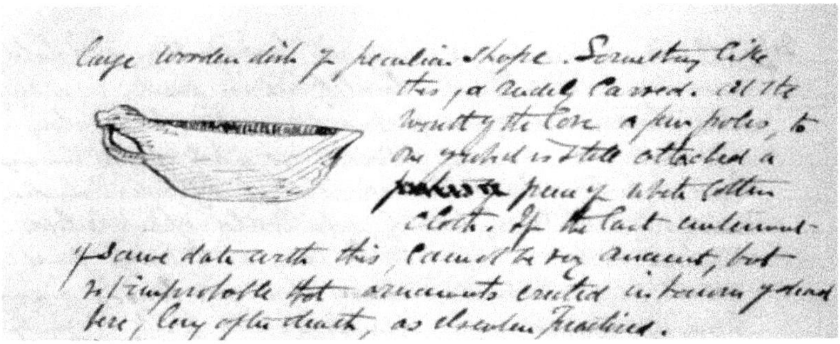

large wooden dish of peculiar shape. Something like this, & rudely carved. At the mouth of the Cove a few poles, to one of which is still attached a piece of white cotton cloth. Of the last [illegible] of same date with this, cannot be very ancient, but [illegible] improbable that ornaments [illegible] in [illegible] [illegible], long after death, as [illegible] practices.

乔治·默瑟·道森绘制的草图，夏洛特皇后群岛调查，1878 年。麦吉尔大学 mg1022 文件 134 第 198 页

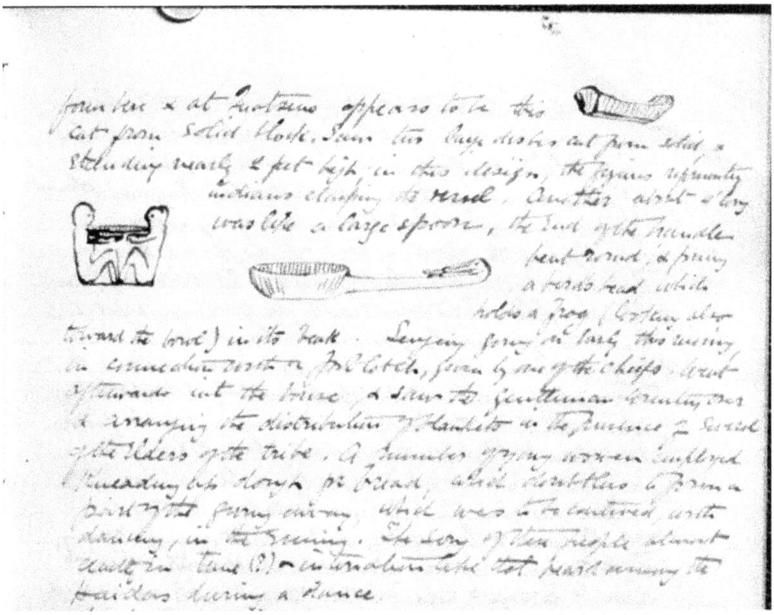

found here & at [illegible] appears to be this cut from solid block. Saw two large dishes cut from solid [illegible] standing nearly 2 feet high in this design, the figures representing Indians clasping the vessel. Another about [illegible] long was like a large spoon, the end of the handle bent round, & [illegible] a bird's head which holds a frog (broken away toward the bowl) in its beak. [illegible] [illegible] [illegible] in connection with [illegible], given by one of the chiefs. Went afterwards into the house & saw the gentleman [illegible] & arranging the distribution of blankets in the presence of several of the elders of the tribe. A number of young women employed threading [illegible] [illegible] [illegible], which doubtless to form a part of the [illegible], which was to be continued with dancing in the evening. The song of these people almost [illegible] in time (?) & intonation like that heard among the Haidas during a dance.

乔治·默瑟·道森的素描，夏洛特皇后群岛调查，1878 年。麦吉尔大学 mg1022 文件 134 第 215 页

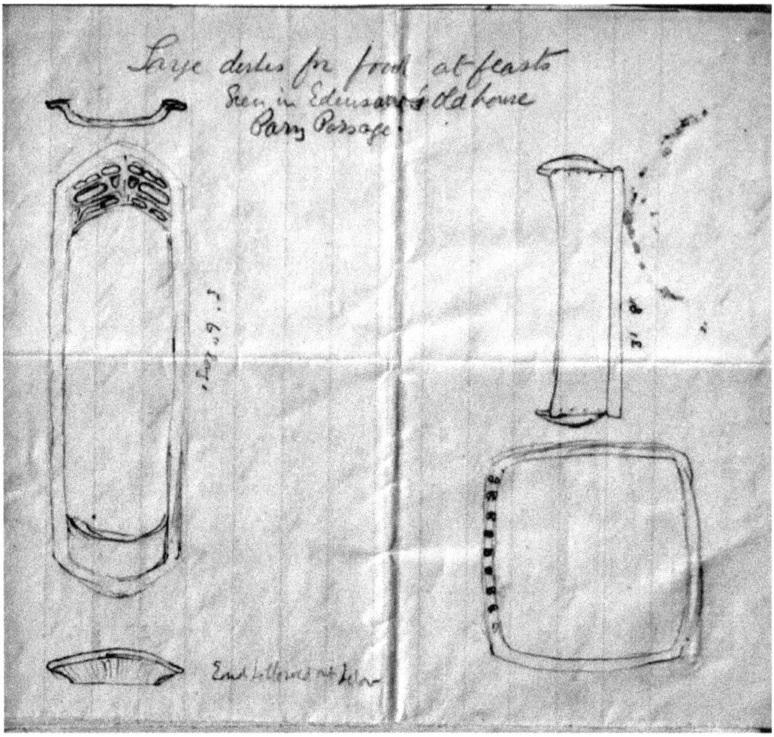

乔治·**默瑟·道森的素描，夏洛特皇后群岛**调查，1878 **年。麦吉**尔大学 mg1022 **文件** 134 **第** 3 页

海达斯

1878 年手写笔记本

作者：乔治·默瑟·道森

原版、完整且未删节

The Haidas

Leaving Victoria, Vancouver Island on the 27th of May 1878, in the little Schooner *Wanderer* of twenty tons burden, we steered North-westward for the Queen Charlotte Islands; & judging our Craft not sufficiently seaworthy for the rough outer Coast of Vancouver Island, exposed to the full sweep of the great North Pacific, we were oblyied to voyage by the inner Channels & wonderful series of Connecting fiords which Characterize the Coast of British Columbia & ramify among its half-submerged mountain ranges. Channels like these however well adapted for steam navigation, & wonderfully picturesque & grand though they are, are tedious enough for sailing vessels.

though they are, are tedious enough for sailing vessels. The wind blows generally either directly up or down the channel, shut in by its mountain walls, & what with calms, & the rapid & constantly changing tidal current, we spent many a weary hour at anchor, or even retrogressing. Sixteen days thus occupied, however, brought us to Milbank Sound, whence, abandoning the idea of visiting first the north end of the islands, we lay across for their southern extremity. In making the traverse of eighty miles we were first becalmed & then, not without some discomfort & danger, weathered half a gale from the north-westward, & on the 12th of June completed our voyage of nearly five hundred miles by casting anchor between the silent wooded shores of a cove in Stewart Channel, which separates Prevost & Moresby Islands.

The object of our expedition was to carry out a preliminary Geological, geographical, & general exploration of the islands, in connection with the Geological Survey of Canada, & in this work we were engaged till the Autumn storms warned us again to seek a more southern latitude. We were furnished, besides provisions for the summer, with dredges & appliances for preserving specimens, photographic requisites & meteorological & other apparatus, with which we were kept busy enough during the season. For the results obtained by these, & with the hammer & compass among the rocks I do not here intend to refer any further, but to present a few details concerning the remarkable

(2)

present a few details concerning the remarkable race of people living on the islands, about whom, though perhaps one of the most interesting native peoples of America, very little accurate information has yet been published.

Within the limits of the Province of British Columbia, in the absence of a trustworthy census, the native races, or 'Indians' are roughly estimated to number 30,000. Tribes associated by language, & collectively belonging to the great Tinneh family, inhabit the whole northern interior of the country. Joining these on the south, & occupying the southern part of the interior are Indians of the Salish connection, divided into many tribes, bearing different names, but all allied in language, the differences between the dialects being generally not so great as to prevent intercommunication. Along the

Coast, & on the outlying islands are scattered a great number of tribes, differing markedly, & in former years frequently hostile one to another. In Customs, modes of life & thought, there is complete diversity between the Coast Indians & those of the interior, a diversity which practically transcends the racial divisions.

In the northern interior, the Indians inhabiting a country for the most part thickly wooded, still remain as they have been heretofore, hunters & fishers, but in many places they now also cultivate small garden patches, where they grow such vegetables as require little attention. For their winter food supply they generally depend chiefly on fish which is dried & cured during the summer. On all the tributaries of the during the Summer. On all the tributaries of the Fraser the Salmon is taken, often in great abundance; & those tribes nearer the coast have generally succeeded in maintaining against the Coast Indians the control of some part of the various smaller rivers, on which Salmon can be caught. Whether they make an annual migration, which they look upon as a sort of holiday-making, revelling during the season in abundance of fresh fish, & on their return carrying back with them a supply for the cold months.

In the southern portion of the interior, the natives have come much more freely in contact with the whites & have already made material progress. In the early days of gold mining labour was in great demand, & consequently every Indian who could or would work was employed at good wages & from this many of them became stock owners in a small way, river boatmen or packers, while others cultivated the soil, sometimes producing more than they required for their own support.

Along the coast, the ~~natives~~ Indians of British Columbia are almost exclusively fishermen. They engage in the chase to a very limited extent & seldom venture far into the dense forests, of which they appear often to entertain a superstitious dread, peopling them in imagination with monsters & fearful inhabitants. ~~Along many of the estuaries & harbours are extensive shell heaps, evidencing the indefinite antiquity of their camping & feasting. At the present day many of the Indians of the Coast are moderately industrious, working on farms, in the coal mines at Nanaimo or as sailors in small coasting vessels~~

While some of these tribes are still little improved, or have been deteriorated from their original condition, others are moderately industrious, ~~the~~ & apply themselves to work in various ways.

various ways.

Sailors in small Coasting vessels

Of the tribes inhabiting the coast, the Haidas are in many respects the most interesting. The Queen Charlotte Islands, which they possess, are separated by wide water stretches ways ~~both~~ from the Archipelago fringing the Coast of the mainland of British Columbia, to the North East, & from the Southern Extremity of Alaska to the North. They form a Compact group, & it is perhaps to their comparative isolation & homogeneity that we owe the fact that the Haidas while remarkably distinct from most other tribes of the coast, are in language & customs so nearly the same in all parts of their own territory. The extreme length of the Queen Charlotte Islands is one hundred & eighty miles, with a greatest breadth of sixty miles.

During Captain Cook's last voyage in the Pacific it was discovered that a lucrative trade in furs might be opened between the North-western Coast of America & China, & though the existence of a part of the Queen Charlotte Islands had been known to the Spaniards since the voyage of Juan Perez, despatched by the Viceroy of Mexico in 1774, it is to the traders who followed in the track of Cook that we owe most of the earlier discoveries on this part of the coast & it is they who appear to have first come in contact with the Haidas. Toward the beginning & during the earlier years of the present century the Queen Charlotte Islands were not infrequently visited by trading vessels. The sea-otter, however, — the skins prized were the most otter, however, — the skins of which were the most valuable articles of trade possessed by the Islanders — having become very scarce through continuous hunting, few vessels but a few coasters have called at any of the ports for many years back. The islands have lain to, on one side of the traffic to ^alaska & the northern part of British Columbia, which of late years has assumed considerable proportions.

The earliest notice of the Haidas which I have been able to find is that given in Captain Dixon's narrative & bears date July 1787. Dixon [illegible] made the land of the islands near their north-western extremity, in the vicinity of North Island, [& gives in the narrative of his voyage a detailed account of his meeting & intercourse with the natives & his trade with them for furs.] he writes:* — "At noon we saw a deep bay which

* A voyage round the World, but more particularly to the North-West Coast of North America. London 1789

bare North-East by East ×× We were determined to make it if possible as there was every probability of meeting with inhabitants. During the night we had light variable winds in every direction, together with a heavy swell from the South West, so that on the morning of the second we found our every effort to reach the bay ineffectual; however, a moderate breeze springing up at North-East, we stood in for the land close by the wind, with our starboard tacks on board. At seven o'clock, to our very great joy, we saw several Canoes full of Indians who appeared to have been out at sea, making towards us. On their coming up with the vessel we found them to be a fishing party, but some of them wore excellent beaver cloaks." They did not seem, however, us. On their coming up with the vessel we found them to be a fishing party, but some of them wore excellent beaver cloaks." They did not seem, however, inclined to dispose of these — " though we endeavoured to tempt them by exhibiting various articles of trade, such as toes, hatchets, adzes, howels, tin-kettles, pans &c. their attention seemed entirely taken up with viewing the vessel, which they apparently did with marks of wonder & surprise. This was looked on as a good omen, & the event showed that for once we were not mistaken. After their curiosity in some measure subsided, they began to trade, & we presently bought what skins & cloaks they had got, in exchange for toes, which they seemed to like very much. They made signs for us to go in towards the shore, & gave us to understand that we should find more inhabitants & plenty of furs. By ten o'clock we were within a mile of the Shore, & saw the village where the Indians dwelt right a-breast of us: it consisted of about six huts which appeared to be built in a more regular form than any we had yet seen; & the situation very pleasant, but the shore was rocky, & afforded no place for us to anchor in. × × During this time several of the people whom we traded with in the morning had been on shore, probably to show their newly acquired bargains, but on seeing us steer for the bay, they presently pushed off after us, joined by several other Canoes. × × A scene now commenced which absolutely beggars all description, & with which we were so overjoyed that we could scarcely believe the evidence of our senses. There were ten believe the Evidence of our senses. There were ten Canoes about the Ship, which contained as nearly as I could estimate one hundred & twenty people; many of these brought most beautiful beaver Cloaks, others excellent skins, & in short, none came empty handed, & the rapidity with which they sold them was a circumstance additionally pleasing; they fairly quarrelled with each other about which should sell his cloak first; & some actually threw their furs on board #, if nobody was at hand to receive them, but we took particular care to let none go from the vessel unpaid. x x In less than half an hour we purchased near three hundred beaver skins* of an excellent quality, a circumstance which greatly raised our spirits."

---

* Though often called beaver skins, as in this place, in Dixon's narrative, the furs obtained were really sea-otter skins, as appears by other evidence. The skins purchased during this voyage, estimated at the prices then ruling at Canton, must have been worth about $90,000

Captain Douglas, the colleague of Meares who is one of the best known of the early voyagers on this coast, visited the same part of the islands a few years later, & gives an interesting account of his dealings with the natives which is, however, too lengthy for insertion here. He is mentioned because on asking the present Chief of that region, Edensaw, for the name of the first white man whom the Haidas had known he at once gave me Douglas, very well known he at once gave me Douglas, very well pronounced. On pressing him, however, he admitted that Douglas may not have been absolutely the first, & it is probably to some still earlier navigator that the story of their first knowledge of the White man preserved by the natives refers.— It was near winter, they say, very long ago, when a ship under sail appeared in the vicinity of North Island. The people were all much afraid, the Chief sharing in the general fear but feeling that it was necessary for the sake of his dignity to act a bold part, he dressed himself in all the finery used in dancing, went out to sea in his Canoe, & performed a Ceremonial dance. It would appear that the childish idea was at first vaguely entertained that the ship was a great bird of some kind, but on approaching it the men on board were seen, & likened from their dark clothing & the general sound & unintelligible character of their talk, to shags — which indeed sometimes look almost human as they sit erect upon the rocks along the border of the sea. It was noticed that one man would speak, whereupon all the others would immediately go aloft, till, something more being said they would as rapidly descend.

When first visited by whites, the population of the islands probably exceeded 7000, at the present day it is ~~I estimate it~~ at about 2000, including in this number many who while now living elsewhere on the coast still call the islands their home.

on the coast still call the islands their home.
In the southern extremity of the Alaskan Archipelago & adjacent to the Queen Charlotte Islands live the Kai-ga-nai Indians numbering about three hundred & in almost every respect the same with the Haidas. They are in fact merely an offshoot from the main stock, for it is to be remarked, that while it might be supposed that traces of the passage of the Haidas to the Queen Charlotte Islands from the mainland would be found, it is known by tradition that the Kai-ga-nai tribe on the contrary migrated to the mainland at a time very remote & in consequence of internecine wars.
The climate of the Queen Charlotte Islands is excessively humid, & they are almost everywhere densely covered with magnificent coniferous trees. Mountains 4000 to 5000 feet high rise in their central portion,

& they are penetrated on all sides by dark deep fiords with rocky walls. To the north east, it is true, a wide stretch of low & nearly level country occurs which may some day support a farming population, but at the present time its sombre woods filled with dense undergrowth & barricaded with prostrate trunks in every stage of decay, offer little to induce either Indian or white to penetrate them. The Haidas therefore, though cultivating here & there along the shores small potato patches, are essentially fishermen. Few paths or trails traverse the interior of the islands, & of these some formerly used when the population was ~~denser~~ greater are now abandoned.

The halibut is found in great abundance in the

The halibut is found in great abundance in the vicinity of the islands, & it is more particularly on this fish that the Haidas depend. Their villages are ~~always~~ invariably situated along the shore, often on bleak wave-lashed parts of the coast, but always in proximity to productive halibut banks. Journeys are made in Canoe along the coast. The Canoes are skilfully hollowed from the great Cedar trees of the region, which after being worked down to a certain ~~degree of thinness~~ small thickness, are steamed, or spread by the insertion of cross pieces till they are made to assume a most graceful form & show lines which would satisfy the most fastidious shipbuilder. In their larger Canoes the Haidas do not hesitate to make long voyages on the open sea, & in former days by their frequent descents on the coast of the mainland, & the facility with which they retreated again to their own islands, rendered themselves more dreaded than any tribe from Vancouver to Sitka.

In their mode of life & the ingenuity & skill which they display in their manufacture of Canoes & other articles, the Haidas do not differ essentially from the other tribes inhabiting the Northern part of the Coast of British Columbia & Southern Alaska. In the Queen Charlotte Islands, however, the peculiar style of architecture & art elsewhere among the Indians of the west Coast more or less prominently exhibited, appears to attain its greatest development. Whether this may show that to the Haidas or their ancestors the introduction of this is due, or indicate merely that with the greater isolation of these people & consequent increased isolation of these people & consequent increased measure of security, the particular ideas of the Indian mind were able to body themselves forth more fully, we may never know. The situation of the islands & the comparative infrequency with which they have been visited for many years, have at least tended to preserve intact many features which have already vanished from the customs & manufactures of most other tribes.

As before stated the permanent villages of the Haidas are invariably situated at the sea shore. They consist generally of a single long row of houses with but a narrow grassy border between it & the beach, on which the canoes of the tribe (for each village constitutes a chieftaincy) are drawn up. In front of each house stands a symbolical carved post, while other carved posts, situated irregularly & differing

Conventional form from those proper to the houses, are generally memorials to the dead. Such a village, seen from a little distance off, the houses & posts grey with the weather, resembles a strip of half burnt forest with dead 'rampikes'. The little cloud of smoke from the various fires may however serve to indicate its true character.

The general type of construction of the houses with the Indians of this part of the N.W. Coast is everywhere nearly the same, but among the Haidas they are more substantially framed, & much more care is given to the fitting together & ornamentation of the edifice than ~~I have~~ is elsewhere seen. The houses are rectangular, & sometimes over forty feet in length of side. The walls are formed of planks split by of side. The walls are formed of planks split by means of wedges from cedar logs & often of great size. The roof is composed of similar split planks, or bark & slopes down at each side, the gable end of the house — if such an expression may be allowed, — facing the sea, towards which the door also opens.

The door is usually an oval hole cut in the base of the grotesquely carved post forty or fifty feet high, which we usually call the totem post, but which to the Haidas is known as Kechen. Stooping to enter one finds that the soil has been excavated in the interior of the house so as to make the actual floor six or eight feet lower than the surface outside. You descend to it by a few rough steps, & on looking about observe that one or two large steps run round all four sides of the house.

These are faced with Cedar planks of great size, which have been hewn out, & serve not only as shelves on which to store all the household goods, but as beds & seats if need be. In the centre of a square area of bare earth, the fire burns, & it will be remarkable if some one of the occupants of the house be not engaged in culinary operations thereat. The smoke mounting upward passes away by what we may call a sky light — an opening in the roof with a shutter to set against the wind, & which serves also as a means of lighting the interior. One is surprised to find what large beams have been employed in framing the house. There are generally four of these laid horizontally, with stout supporting

four others laid horizontally, with stout supporting uprights at the Ends. They are really hewn & of a symmetrical cylindrical form & are generally fitted into the hollowed Ends of the uprights thus.

This form of joint seems to recommend itself particularly to the Indian constructive idea everywhere, though scarcely such as would be chosen by one of our Carpenters. The uprights are often about fifteen feet high, with a diameter of about three feet, & it is only when we become acquainted with the fact that a regular _bee_ is held at the erection of the house, that we can account for the movement without machinery of such large logs. The bee is accompanied by a distribution of property on the part of the man for whom the house is being built, well known on the West Coast by the Chinook name _potlatch_. Such a house as this accommodates several families in one house of the kind, each occupying a certain corner or portion of the interior.

We must return, however, to the carved posts, which constitute the most distinctive feature of a Haida village. To make one of these a large & sound cedar tree, probably three or four feet in diameter, is chosen somewhere not far from the waters edge, felled, trimmed, & then moved down to the sea. Being launched it is towed to the village site, & by united labour dragged up above high water mark on the beach. It is then shaped & carved, some of the Indians being famous for their skill in this business & earning considerable sums by practising it. The log is hollowed behind like a trough, to make it. The log is hollowed behind like a trough, to make it light, while the front is generally covered with a mass of grotesque figures in which the animal representing the totem or Clan of the person for whom it is made takes a prominent place. It constitutes in fact his coat of arms, & may in some instances be gaily painted. When all is finished the post is taken to its place & firmly planted in the ground, to remain a thing of beauty till under the influence of the Climate it becomes grey with age, & hoary with moss & lichen.

The peculiar type of art most fully displayed on the carved posts is found more or less in all the manufactures of the Haidas. The neat & even elegant wooden dishes, which formerly served all household purposes, embody always some peculiar animal form or grouping of forms more or less complicated or contorted. Though the artist may be able to copy nature faithfully enough when he tries, as witnessed in some of the masks used in dancing, he in most cases prefers to follow certain conventional ideas which appear by long usage to have become incorporated with the native mind.

Not the least curious of the customs of the Haidas, & probably with some religious significance, are those connected with dancing ceremonies. It is remarkable too that most of these are said to have been derived from the Tshimsians of the neighbouring mainland, a people speaking a language quite distinct, & till within a few years generally at bitter war with the Haidas. The dancing ceremonies are divided, so far as I have been able to learn, into six classes, known respectively as Skā-ga, Ska-dul, [illegible]

These appear to be divided into six classes which are designated by as many unpronounceable names as necessary have to set down.

known respectively as Skā-ga, Ska-dul, Kwai-o-guns-o-lung, Ka-ta-ka-gun, Ska-dut & Hi-atl.

Often I have been fortunate enough to see one, the Kwai-o-guns-o-lung, a description of which, given nearly as written down at the time, may serve to illustrate a Class of [performances] Ceremonies once common among the native peoples, but which have now almost everywhere passed away. —

Landing after dark from our boat at the southern end of the fine sandy beach on which Skidegate village fronts, we found this part of the town apparently quite deserted, but could discern a dim glow of light at a distance, & distinguish the monotonous

Sound of the drums. Scrambling as best we might in the dark by the path which zig-zags along the front of the row of houses & narrowly escaping falls over various obstacles, we reached the house in which the dance was going on. The door was here a little on one side of the middle of the front, & did not open through the base of the carved post as is generally the case with the older fashioned buildings. Pushing it [the door] open, a glare of light flashed out, which had previously been seen only as it filtered through the various crevices of the house; & entering we found ourselves behind & among the dancers who stood within the house with their backs to the front wall. Edging through them we crossed the open space in which the fire — well supplied with space in which the fire — well supplied with resinous logs — was burning, & seated ourselves on the floor amidst a crowd of onlookers at the further end. The house was of the usual oblong shape, but was not excavated in the centre, as is often the case, but on a level with the ground outside. The floor [heavy] was covered with cedar planks with the exception of a square space in the centre for the fire, & the goods & chattels of the family were piled here & there in heaps along the walls, leaving the greater part of the interior clear.

The dancers, as already stated, occupied the front end of the building while the audience [was arranged] disposed themselves along the sides & at the further end, [illegible] filling almost every available space, squatting in various attitudes on the floor, & consisting of men women & children of all ages. The smoke of the fire escaped by wide openings in the roof without causing any inconvenience & its glow brightly illuminated the faces & forms of all present. The performers, in this instance about twenty in number, were dressed according to no uniform plan, but attired in their best clothes — or at least their most showy ones — with the addition of certain ornaments & badges appropriate to the occasion. All, or nearly all, wore head-dresses variously constructed of twisted cedar bark & ornamented with feathers, or, as in one case with a bristling circle of the whiskers of the sea-lion. Shoulder-girdles made of cedar bark coloured or girdles made of Cedar bark coloured or ornamented with tassels were very common. One man wore leggins covered with fringes of puffin beaks strung together, which rattled as he moved. Many, if not all, held sprigs of fresh spruce in the hand, & were covered about the head with downy feathers, which also floated in abundance in the warm air of the ~~[illegible]~~ house. Some had rattles, & added to the din by shaking these furiously at the accentuated parts of the song. Five women took part in the dance, standing in front in a row & were dressed with some uniformity, several having the peculiarly valuable Cedarbark & goats-wool shawls made by the Tshimsians. The head-dresses of the women were all alike, consisting in each case of a small mask or semblance of a face carved neatly in wood, & inlaid with pearly haliotis shell. These attached to a cedar bark erection & built round with gay feathers & tassels, stood before the forehead, while at the back, in some cases, depended a train with ermine skins. The faces of both men & women engaged in the dance were gaily painted, vermilion being the favourite colour.

One man, acting as master of the Ceremonies, stood in the middle of the back row of performers slightly higher than the rest. He was dressed almost altogether in white, & held in his hand a long wand with which he kept time & led off the singing. A second man held a white stick with a split &

altogether in White, & held in his hand a long wand with which he kept time & led off the singing. A second man held a white stick with a split & trimmed feather at the top. He occupied a prominent place at one side, in the front row of dancers, & seemed to speak in a recitative voice at times when the others merely gave utterance to meaningless sounds.

The performer on the drum, — a flat tambourine-like article formed of hide stretched on a hoop — sat opposite the dancers & near the fire, so that they could mutually see each others movements. The drum was beaten very regularly with double knocks, thus — tum tum — tum tum — tum tum — & with the sound the dancers kept time in a sort of chant or song to which words are set, & which swells into a full chorus or dies away according to the motions of the ~~master of the ceremonies~~ [a leader who stays among the dancers], as I

~~have called him~~, who besides marking time with them ~~stops to~~ gave a few words of direction or exhortation. To the drumming & singing the dancing also keeps time, following it very closely. At every beat a spasmodic twitch passes through the crowd of dancers, who scarcely ~~raise~~ lift their feet from the floor but move by double jerks, shuffling the feet a little at the same time. Those who dance best — especially the women before referred to — turn about half round in three or four jerks & then turn back again in the next three or four. These women also allow their heads to move as though loosely supported on pivots, nodding idiotically as they shuffle about. When the chorus swells to as they shuffle about. When the chorus swells to *forte*, the rattles are plied with tenfold vigour & the din becomes very great. After the performance has continued for ten minutes or so the the master of the Ceremonies gives a sign & all suddenly stop with a loud *hugh*! The dance is again resumed by the perspiring crowd, at the signal of the drum, which strikes up after a few moments rest has been allowed.

The crowd of gaily painted gaily dressed savages by the kind light of the fire presented on the whole a rather brave & imposing appearance, & when excited in the dance the Haida may yet almost imagine the grand old days to remain when hundreds crowded the villages now occupied by tens, & nothing had eclipsed the grandeur of their Ceremonies & doings.

of Stories connected with localities, or accounting for various circumstances, there are no doubt very many among the Haidas. Of these a few I have been able to collect ~~a few~~. The fundamental narrative of the origin of man & the beginning of the present state of affairs is the most important of their myths. ~~This, as given~~ below is I believe in all its main points correct, that is to say unaltered from its original traditional form. Minor shades of meaning may in some cases be indefinite, as it was obtained through the medium of the Chinook, aided by what little English my informant was master of. —

Very long ago, they say, there was a great flood by which all

[illegible]

Very long ago, they say, there was a great flood by which all men & animals were destroyed, with the exception of a single raven. This creature was not, however, exactly an ordinary bird, but — as with all animals in the old Indian stories — possessed the attributes of a human being to a great extent. His coat of feathers, for instance, could be put on or taken off at will like a garment. It is even related in one version of the story that he was born of a woman who had no husband, & that she made bows & arrows for him. With these, when old enough, he killed birds, & of the skins she sewed a cape or blanket. The birds were: the little snow-bird with black head & neck, the large black & red woodpecker, & the Mexican woodpecker. The name of this being was <u>Ne-kil-sttas</u>.

When the flood had gone down <u>Ne-kil-sttas</u>

looked about, but could find neither companion nor a mate, & became very lonely. At last he took a cockle shell from the beach, & marrying it, he constantly continued to brood & think earnestly of his wish for a companion. By & bye in the shell he heard a very faint cry like ~~that~~ of a newly born child, but which gradually became louder, till at last a little female child was seen, which growing by degrees larger & larger was finally married by the raven, & from this union all the Indians were produced & the country peopled. The people, however, had many wants, & as yet had neither fire, daylight, fresh water, or the oolachen fish. These things were all in the possession of a great Chief or deity called

possession of a great Chief or deity called
Settin-Ki-jash, who lived where the Nasse River
now is. Water was first obtained by Ne-kil-sttas
in the following manner. The Chief had a daughter,
& to her Ne-kil-sttas covertly made love, &
visited her many times unknown to her father.
The girl began to love Ne-kil-sttas very much
& trust in him, which was what he desired,
& at length when he thought the time ripe, he asked
on one occasion for a drink of water, saying
that he was very thirsty. The girl brought him
the water in one of the closely woven baskets in
common use, but he drank only a little, & setting
the basket down [for that purpose] beside him waited till the girl
fell asleep. Then quickly donning his coat of
feathers, & lifting the basket in his beak, he flew

out by the opening made for the smoke in the top of the lodge. He was in great haste, fearing to be followed by the people of the Chief, & a little water fell out here & there causing the numerous rivers which are now found, but on the Haida country a few drops only fell, like rain, & so it is that there are no large streams there to this day.

Ne-kil-stlas next wished to obtain fire, which was also in the possession of the same powerful being or Chief. He did not dare, however, to appear again in the Chief's house, nor did the Chief's daughter longer show him favour. Assuming therefore the form of a single needle-like leaf of the spruce tree he floated on the water near the

[illegible]
the spruce tree he floated on the water near the house, & when the girl — his former lover — came down to draw water, was lifted by her in the vessel she used. The girl drinking the water swallowed without noticing it the little leaf & shortly afterwards bore a child who was no other than the cunning Ne-kil-stlas, who had thus again obtained an entry into the lodge. Watching his opportunity, he one day picked up a burning brand, & flying out as before by the smoke-hole at the top of the lodge, carried it away & spread fire everywhere.

All this time, however, the people were without daylight, & it was next the object of Ne-kil-stlas to obtain this for them. This time he tried still another plan. He pretended that he also had light, & continued to assert it though the chief denied

Similar childish stories serve to explain the origin of light & the prized oolachen fish.

the truth of his statement. He, however, in some way made an object bearing a resemblance to the moon, which, while all the people were out fishing on the sea in the perpetual night, he allowed to be partly seen from under his coat of feathers. It cast a faint glimmer across the waters, which the people & Setlin-Ki-jash thought was caused by a veritable moon. Disgusted at finding he was not the sole possessor of light, & loosing all conceit of his property, the great chief immediately placed the sun & moon where we now see them.

One thing more, much desired, still remained in the possession of Setlin-Ki-jash — the oolachen, a little fish highly prized by the Indians of the North-west Coast as a source of edible oil. Now

North-west Coast as a source of edible oil. Now the Shag was a friend and companion of the Chief & had access to his property, including his store of oolachens. Ne-kil-sttas contrived that the sea-gull & the Shag should quarrel, by telling each that the other had spoken ill of him. At last he got them together, when, after an angry conversation they followed his advice & began to fight. Ne-kil-sttas knew that the Shag had an oolachen in his stomach & so urged the combatants to fight harder & to lie on their backs & strike out with their feet. This they did, & finally the Shag threw up the oolachen, which Ne-kil-sttas immediately seized. Making a canoe from a rotten log, he smeared it & himself with the scales of the oolachen, & then coming at night near the great Chief's lodge said that he was very cold & wished to come in & warm himself, as he had been making a great catch of oolachens which he had left somewhere not far off. Setten-ke-jash said that this could not be true as he only possessed the fish, but Ne-kilstlas invited the Chief to look at his clothes & at his canoe. Finding both covered with scales the Chief became convinced that oolachens besides those which he had must exist, & again in disgust at finding he had not the monopoly he turned all the oolachens loose, saying, at the same time, that every year they would come in vast numbers & continue to show his liberality & be a monument to him. This they have never failed to do since that time.

have never failed to do since that time.

This Haida story of the origin of things is substantially the same with that which I have been told by Indians of the Tsimsh stock in the northern part of the interior of British Columbia. My surprise on hearing it gradually unfolded as a Haida myth, was very great. It would be hazardous to theorise on the cause of this similarity in tribes so distant & so dissimilar in habits, but it is certain that both its versions are derived from a common source not very remote. As is always the case with these aboriginal stories a local colouring has been given to the narrative by the Haidas, & the story of the oolachen is an addition to that which I have heard from the Tsimsh. It shows the great value set on this fish that it should be classed among the primary necessaries of existence, Such as light, water & fire.

Ne-kil-sttas of the Haidas is represented in function & name by Us-tas of the Carrier Dinneh. Of Us-tas an almost endless series of grotesque & often disgusting adventures are related, & analogous tales are reported about Ne-kil-sttas. One of these sets forth that having disguised himself as a dead raven, & floating upon the surface of the sea, he was swallowed by a whale, which, by violent pains being then induced to strand himself became a prey to the Haidas, invisible Ne-kil-sttas meanwhile walking out of the whale's belly at the proper moment.

The collection & study of

Such details as ~~these~~ are above given concerning the habits customs & thoughts of a people semi-barbarous,

The collection & study of → Such details as ~~these~~ are these above given concerning the habits customs & thoughts of a people semi-barbarous, & disappearing even before our eyes in the universal menstruum of Civilization, may seem to be of little importance. They lead, however, into a wide & interesting region of speculation, embracing the question of the origin & interrelation of the American aborigines, their wanderings, & all the unwritten pages of their history, which we can hope to know ~~[illegible]~~ even by the most careful enquiry, only in dim outlines. We are led to ask ourselves in particular, in regard to the Haidas, what has been the origin of the grotesque but highly conventionalized art which exists itself in many of the works of these people, & the social customs, which exert a power almost as strong as that of fashion among ourselves.

Causes them to devote so much of their time to ceremonies apparently meaningless but which serve to form the bonds & rough working machinery of Society among them. Have these been those of a people who —

"Flying, found shelter in the Fortunate Isles,
And left their usages, their arts & laws.
To disappear by a slow gradual death,
To dwindle & to perish one by one
Starved in those narrow bounds."

or have they been developed slowly in a community separated from the human stock at a very early period, & might they, — had they never been brought face to face with a superior power — have grown in the course of ages into an independant civilization the course of ages into an independant civilization like that of Mexico or Peru.? We can never hope to answer such questions fully, but in regard to these people of the North-west Coast, we know that there are on record several instances in which Japanese junks driven by the prevailing winds & currents have been carried across the whole breadth of the North Pacific, and that the passage across Behring's Strait to the North is short, & is even occasionally at the present day made on the winter ice by the Esquimaux.

It is therefore more than probable that peoples with their rude arts, may from time to time have been borne to the western coast of America, & that it is to Eastern Asia that we must look for the origin of its [substantial] peoples.

One question at least, of a practical character must be answered for the Haidas & other similarly situated tribes of the North-west Coast. What is to be done with them? It is probable that they have already nearly reached that critical point of their first contact with the whites, beyond which they cease to diminish, & may begin to increase in numbers. It would be a mistake to attempt to bring these people back into a state of tutelage such as that which has resulted in keeping some of our Eastern Indians in a condition nearly stationary, with regard to civilization, for a period of one or two hundred years. They do not require reserves two hundred years. They do not require reserves of arable land, for though having strict ideas of their proprietary right in their native islands they are essentially fishermen. Some amicable arrangement must, in the first instance be come to for the land, while the people are taught to cure their fish in such a way that it will have a merchantable value, instructed to become artisans — for in handicraft the Haidas show a special aptitude — & encouraged to become sailors. —

George M. Dawson.

参考文献

Haidas 的原始笔记本可在以下位置查看：麦吉尔大学档案馆，魁北克省蒙特利尔，Dawson-Harrington 档案 MG1022。https://digitalarchives.library.mcgill.ca/MUA/MG1022/series6/mua_dawson_fonds_MUAMG1022-6-104.pdf 文章的约 70% 经过轻微编辑后发表在 Harper's New Monthly Magazine 上。1882 年，George Mercer Dawson 的《Haidas》。 P. [401]-408：插图。 EN ISBN：0665148577， 9780665148576。Harper 的 CIHM/ICMH 缩微胶片可在以下网址查看：https://ia600208.us.archive.org/31/items/cihm_14857/cihm_14857.pdf 夏洛特皇后群岛报告 作者 George M Dawson 1849-1901。 印刷书籍 1880 蒙特利尔：加拿大地质调查局， ISBN：9780665036569，0665036566 OCLC 编号/唯一标识符：606215347 https://bac-lac.on.worldcat.org/ oclc/606215347?lang=en 和 https://open.library.ubc.ca/collections/bcbooks/items/1.0222501 物理描述：v, 239B 页，14 页图版 插入三张折叠地图。附有以下附录：A. 关于夏洛特皇后群岛的海达印第安人。 身体特征和服饰 食物 社会组织 宗教和医学 Potlach，或财产分配 舞蹈仪式 社会习俗 艺术和建筑 传统和民间传说 与欧洲人的第一次接触——毛皮贸易 村庄 人口 B. 海达印第安人的词汇 A 和 B 也可以在以下网址查看：https://www.canadiana.ca/view/oocihm.14877/3 GMD 在 1878 年调查夏洛特皇后群岛期间撰写的单独笔记本，包括草图，可以在以下网址查看：https://digitalarchives.library.mcgill.ca/MUA/MG1022/mua_george-mercer-dawson-diary_1878_envelope-49_MG1022.pdf